WESTCHESTER PUBLIC LIB.

W9-BAJ-267

WHY SHOULD I GET OFF THE COUCH?

✦ and other questions about health and exercise ✦

Louise Spilsbury

Heinemann Library
Chicago, Illinois

© 2003 Heinemann Library,
a division of Reed Elsevier Inc.
Chicago, Illinois

Customer Service 888-454-2279

Visit our website at www.heinemannlibrary.com

All rights reserved. No part of this publication may be reproduced or transmitted in any form or by any means, electronic or mechanical, including photocopying, recording, taping, or any information storage and retrieval system, without permission in writing from the publisher.

Designed by David Poole and Tokay Interactive Ltd
Illustrations by Kamae Design Ltd
Qriginated by Ambassador Litho Ltd
Printed in China by WKT

07 06
10 9 8 7 6 5 4 3 2

Library of Congress Cataloging-in-Publication Data
Spilsbury, Louise.
  Why should I get off the couch? : and other questions about health and exercise / Louise Spilsbury.
      v. cm. -- (Body matters)
Includes bibliographical references and index.
Contents: Why should I get off the couch? -- Why is it bad to be unfit?
-- What kind of exercise is best? -- Why should I do warm-ups? -- Why do
cool-downs after exercise? -- How often should I exercise? -- Why should
I wear trainers? -- Should I eat special food? -- Why does exercise hurt
sometimes? -- What if I don't like team sports? -- What if it's raining
outside?
  ISBN 1-4034-4681-4 (HC)
  1. Exercise--Juvenile literature. 2. Children--Health and
hygiene--Juvenile literature. [1. Exercise. 2. Health.] I. Title. II.
Series.
  RA781.S65 2003
  613.7'1--dc21

                                  2003004884

Acknowledgments
p. 4 Robert Harding; p. 5 Corbis/Paul A. Souders; p. 6 Getty Images/Imagebank; pp. 7, 12, 13, 17, 23, 28 Tudor Photography; pp. 8, 20 Corbis/Ariel Skelly; pp. 9, 11 Getty Images/Stone; p. 14 Corbis/Sygma: Orban Thierry; p. 15 Corbis/Gim Craigmyle; pp. 16, 21 Getty Images/Taxi; pp. 18, 19, 24 Photodisc; p. 22 Science Photo Library; p. 25 Corbis/Tom & Dee Ann McCarthy; pp. 26, 27 Corbis/Tom Stewart.

Cover photograph by Alamy/Corbis.

Every effort has been made to contact copyright holders of any material reproduced in this book. Any omissions will be rectified in subsequent printings if notice is given to the publisher.

Some words are shown in bold, **like this.** You can find out what they mean by looking in the glossary.

CONTENTS

Keep a diary

Throughout the book, there are ideas for keeping a diary—a record of the exercises you do and how they help you. You can add your own notes to the diary, too.

WHY SHOULD I GET OFF THE COUCH?

If you leave a battery-operated toy switched on, buzzing gently in your bedroom, it runs down. If you leave your bicycle unused in the garage for too long, it gets rusty and the tires go flat. If you spend too long on the couch, you will run down, too!

Making muscles

You have **muscles** all over your body. Some, such as those in your arms and legs, help you to move. Another muscle, your **diaphragm,** helps you breathe. Your **heart** is a special muscle that pumps blood around your body. When you exercise, you make your muscles stronger. This means that they can keep you going for longer and are less likely to get damaged.

This gymnast knows how important it is to stretch and move his body! If you do not exercise your muscles, **bones,** and **joints** regularly, they will not move so well and may get stiff.

Weighty matters

When you eat, your body converts some of the **nutrients** in the food into **energy.** You need energy for everything you do, from breathing to biking. If you eat a lot and do not get much exercise, you will get more fuel from your food than you actually need. Your body will store the extra fuel as fat, and you will put on weight.

The feel-good factor

Getting off the couch can make you feel good, too. If you have had a bad day at school or a fight with a friend, exercise can help you feel better. Exercise makes you feel more positive and more confident about yourself and your body.

It is not just winning the trophy that makes this team so happy. Exercise can make your body release **endorphins**—chemicals that actually make you feel happier.

WHY IS IT BAD TO BE UNFIT?

When you are unfit, or out of shape, your body will not work as well and may become unhealthy. Exercising helps keep your whole body in good working order. The most important part of your body is your **heart,** and exercise is a surefire way to keep your heart healthy and happy.

Have you noticed that your heart beats faster when you exercise? When you stop, you can feel it beating at top speed.

HOW DOES MY HEART WORK?

Your heart is found in your chest. It is about the size of a fist. Its walls are made of solid **muscle.** This muscle contracts (tightens) the heart to squeeze blood into the **blood vessels** which carry blood around the body. Blood from the heart carries oxygen to your body parts, which they need in order to work.

Keep a diary

Your pulse rate is how many times your heart beats in a minute. It goes up when you exercise. The fitter you are, the quicker it returns to normal afterward.

- Take your pulse and write it down. Take it again after running for two minutes. How long before it is back to normal?
- Exercise regularly for two weeks. Do the same test as before. Has your recovery time—and, therefore, your fitness—improved?

An easy place to take your pulse is the main **artery** in your wrist. Place the first two fingers of one hand on the inside of your other wrist, lining up with your thumb. Count how many beats you feel in 15 seconds, then multiply this number by four. This is your pulse rate.

Why does my heart race when I exercise?

When you exercise, your muscles work harder. When they work harder, they need more **oxygen** and **nutrients** to keep them going. You feel your heart beating faster in your chest because it is working harder, too. It is pumping more blood—which carries oxygen and nutrients to the muscles.

WHAT KIND OF EXERCISE IS BEST?

HOW DO MUSCLES WORK?

Muscles are made of hundreds of small fibers that are elastic (a little like rubber bands). Muscles are attached to **bones** by **tendons,** which are a little like ropes. When you contract (tighten) a muscle, the tendons move, pulling the bones with them.

The best kind of exercise is the one you enjoy most because if you like doing it you will keep going back for more! Most activities are good for you, but different kinds of exercise help you in different ways. It is best to do a variety of things to make sure that you increase your strength, stamina, and flexibility.

Exercise for strength

Exercise is important for keeping your **muscles** strong. When you exercise regularly, you increase the size and strength of your muscles. Strong muscles help you do all the things you want to.

Paddling a canoe is good for your arm muscles—and lots of fun, too!

Activities such as running and biking are great for building strong, hardworking leg muscles. Rowing, push-ups, and tennis are good for your arms. Some kinds of exercise, such as swimming, help many muscles at once.

Exercise for stamina

When your **heart** and **lungs** are stronger, you have more stamina. This means you can be active for longer without getting worn out.

Aerobic exercises build up your heart and lungs. Aerobic means "needing **oxygen.**" Aerobic exercises, such as running, soccer, dancing, and biking, make you breathe hard to get the extra oxygen your muscles need to keep going. This gives your lungs and heart a workout—your lungs breathe deeply and more quickly, and your heart pumps faster to send more oxygen in the blood to your muscles.

When you swim, you breathe harder, and that gives your heart and lungs some well-needed exercise.

WHY SHOULD I CARE ABOUT MY JOINTS?

Without joints, you would not be able to move! Joints are where your bones meet, and they allow your bones to move. You have joints at your elbows, knees, ankles, shoulders and many other places.

Exercise for flexibility

Being flexible means that your body can stretch and bend easily. Most young people are naturally flexible—they can touch their toes and bend without much trouble. As people get older, they often become less flexible. This is because their **joints** become stiffer and their **muscles** become weaker—usually because they do not get enough exercise.

To keep your body flexible, try doing activities in which you have to bend and stretch your body. Dancing, gymnastics, and martial arts are a few examples.

You do not need to become a gymnast to get flexible! Just try some easy indoor exercises, such as gentle stretching and bending, to keep yourself loose.

It does not matter whether your team wins or loses a game. The important things about team sports are exercising, enjoying yourself, and making friends.

What is so good about team sports?

Football, baseball, basketball, hockey, soccer—the list of team sports is long. What is so good about them? When you play for a team, you do much more than build up your strength, stamina, and flexibilty. Cooperating with teammates is a good lesson in working with others and a great way to make new friends. Everyone shares the team's successes and disappointments.

Keep a diary

- In your diary, keep a record of what kinds of exercise you do each day for two weeks.
- Note whether you think it helped your strength, stamina, or flexibility. (Some activities— such as swimming—do all three!)
- Which kind of exercise do you do most? Which do you enjoy most?

11

WHY SHOULD I DO WARM-UPS?

Although **muscles** and **tendons** are pretty strong, you can hurt them if you suddenly start pulling and twisting them before they have been warmed up. The pain usually only lasts a little while, but you can avoid it altogether if you spend some time doing warm-up exercises first.

Preparing for action!

Doing warm-ups raises the temperature of the **cells** in your body, which increases their activity rate. Warm-ups also increase the supply of blood to the muscles, which brings more **oxygen** and **nutrients** to give them **energy.** They also release fluids around the **joints** in your body so that they move more smoothly.

Warm-ups reduce the chances of muscle strain—when you tear some of the tiny muscle fibers, leaving your muscle sore and tender. Warm-ups make your muscles and tendons more elastic and flexible.

Which warm-ups are best?

The best warm-ups to do first start you off fairly gently. Brisk walking and slow jogging are good activities to get your blood flowing. Then try stretching different parts of your body to loosen up the joints and warm up the muscles. Slowly stretch a body part, such as an arm or leg, and hold that stretch for 20 seconds. (Never stretch so far that it hurts and never bounce while stretching.) Finally, do something a bit more energetic, such as a short, fast run, to get yourself ready for action.

Toe touches are a good stretching exercise. Stand straight with your feet slightly apart and arms stretched out to the sides. Twist your body (keeping your arms straight) and touch your left toes with your right hand and then your right toes with your left hand.

13

WHY DO COOL-DOWNS AFTER EXERCISE?

When a winning athlete jogs gently around the track after a race, she is not just enjoying a moment of glory. Gentle jogging is also a form of cooling down— a way of making sure that the body winds down properly after exercise.

Slowing down

Cool-downs allow your body temperature, breathing, and **heart** rate to return to normal gradually. It is especially important to let your heartbeat get back to its regular rate for it to function properly. If you stop exercise suddenly, blood in your body may stay around your leg **muscles** instead of returning to the heart and brain. This can make you feel light-headed or dizzy.

Exercise can make you hot, but if you stop suddenly, you can get very cold—and even catch a chill. Cool-downs help you cool down gradually and safely.

14

Cool-downs also help the rest of your body get back to normal slowly rather than suddenly. Flopping into a chair right after exercising can make your muscles ache. Cool-downs help your muscles loosen up again gradually after they have tightened during exercise.

Cool-downs do not have to be complicated. Taking five minutes to walk and talk with a friend is a good cool-down.

Which cool-downs should I do?

The idea of cool-downs is to let your body slow down by keeping slightly active, say with a brisk walk or gentle jogging. Try to gently stretch all your muscles, particularly those you used most for the exercise. Shake your arms and legs. Bend your neck and back. You can do the same kind of stretching exercises that you use for warm-ups. You should spend about five minutes on your cool-downs.

HOW OFTEN SHOULD I EXERCISE?

By doing a chore, such as washing the car, you will not only get fitter —you will also earn brownie points with your parents.

You should try to do some kind of **aerobic exercise** at least two or three times a week for 20 to 30 minutes at a time. When you think that this includes gym class and recess at school, it is not really all that much. Even dancing and playing hopscotch are aerobic activities.

Find the time

If you have trouble making time for exercise, fit it into your schedule in other ways, perhaps by walking or biking to school instead of getting a ride. Walk up the stairs instead of using escalators or elevators. Help out with some household chores such as vacuuming the carpets or digging in the garden.

16

Can I get too much exercise?

Some people say that you cannot have too much of a good thing. With exercise, though, you can. If you suddenly start running long distances or playing soccer all day, you may end up in pain. Feeling weak, dizzy, or sick may also be signs that you have done too much. Exercise gradually, building up the amount you do each week, until your body is ready to do more. Do not overdo exercise—just make it a regular part of your life.

Keep a diary

- Keep a record of the amount of exercise you do every week for six weeks. Include the time it takes to walk to school. If you play tag, kickball, or football at recess, include that time, too.
- How much exercise did you do in a week?

Do not worry about how much distance you cover when you exercise—the important thing is to enjoy it.

WHY SHOULD I WEAR SNEAKERS?

Why does it matter what you wear when you exercise? The right gear allows you to move easily and can protect your body from bumps.

The right stuff

For most sports, shorts, a T-shirt, and a pair of sneakers are all you need, but some sports require special gear. For example, swimsuits are extra stretchy, so they are easy to move in.

When you run, your feet hit the ground hard. Sneakers have padded soles that absorb the shock so that your feet do not have to.

You also need to make sure that you wear the right footwear for the exercise you do. Baseball shoes have cleats in the bottom to grip the ground, and tennis shoes are shaped to support the arch of your feet and your ankles as you twist and spin on the court.

Protecting your eyes

If you play a sport where there is a risk of your eyes getting hit by an object such as a ball, you should wear some form of eye protection, such as goggles or a guard that fits to a helmet. Ice hockey players wear helmets to protect their eyes and the rest of their head, and baseball catchers wear face masks along with other protective gear.

Wearing the right protective gear is not just for beginners. The world's top swimmers wear goggles when they race.

Helmets and pads

Your head houses a very important part of your body—your brain. Your skull does its best to protect the brain, but if you play sports where there is a risk of falling on or bumping your head, you need a helmet. You should, for example, wear a helmet while riding a bike, a horse, or a scooter, and when you go in-line skating or skateboarding.

You can wear pads to protect other parts of your body when biking, skating, or playing sports such as football, soccer, and hockey. Pads are like cushions that you strap tightly to elbows, shins, and knees. They protect your skin and the **bones, joints,** and **muscles** beneath the skin from being broken or bruised.

When choosing a bike helmet, make sure you get one that is the right size so that it does not slide around. Always wear it on top of your head, not tilted back.

SHOULD I EAT SPECIAL FOOD?

Commercials often show athletes with special food and drinks, trying to convince you that they can make you fitter and faster. In fact, all you need to do is to eat the right amount of a variety of foods to keep fueled-up for fun.

Bananas are a good energy snack, but do not eat anything less than one hour before a game, because it might make you feel sick.

Food for fitness

To be healthy, we all need to eat the right balance of the four different types of food—**carbohydrates,** fruit and vegetables, **proteins,** and fatty or sugary foods. Carbohydrates, such as pasta and bread, give you **energy.** Try to eat some carbohydrates at every meal. Fruit and vegetables are excellent sources of **vitamins,** which help you grow and protect you from illness. Try to eat at least five different kinds every day.

21

You need **protein**-rich foods, such as meat, fish, eggs, milk, and beans, to grow strong and keep well, but you only need small amounts. Your body also needs small amounts of fatty foods, such as oil or butter, to give you **energy** and help your **cells** form properly.

Water works

Dehydration is dangerous, so always pack a bottle of water in your backpack along with your sneakers!

You need to drink water every day, but you always need more when you exercise. When you are active, especially in hot weather, you **sweat.** Your body cools itself by releasing water through the **sweat glands** in your skin. If you do not replace the water you lose, you get **dehydrated.** This does not just mean that you feel really thirsty. Your body needs water to work properly. If you get dehydrated, you may feel dizzy, weak, or sick.

WHY DOES EXERCISE HURT SOMETIMES?

Our bodies use pain to tell us things. When exercise hurts, it is your body's way of telling you that something is wrong! If you feel pain when you exercise, stop and get it checked out.

Stitches and cramps

Stitches and cramps hit suddenly but are not really serious. A stitch is a sharp, stabbing pain in the side which people often get when they run soon after eating. **Oxygen** goes to the leg **muscles,** and the stomach muscles do not get enough oxygen to **digest** the food, so they hurt. A cramp happens when a muscle suddenly starts tightening by itself. It can happen when you work a muscle too hard.

Muscles may ache after exercise if you have not exercised for a while. This is not necessarily bad pain. Rubbing and gently stretching should make the muscles feel better.

23

Serious damage?

Sometimes a pain is more serious, such as a broken **bone** or a damaged **muscle.** When you have a pain that does not go away completely after a few minutes, ask an adult to look at it. You should also ask for help if you feel dizzy or sick or have a headache.

Getting breathless

You breathe faster when you exercise because your body needs to get extra **oxygen** to your muscles. Remember to breathe properly during exercise—always breathe in through your nose and out through your mouth, and never hold your breath. If you start panting and feel really out of breath, take a break. If you exercise too hard or fast, you may end up feeling dizzy or sick.

Do not let the risk of getting hurt discourage you—few people your age get hurt doing exercise. In fact, you are more likely to have health problems if you do not exercise.

PAIN PREVENTION

Here are some tips for things you can do to avoid injuries when you exercise.

- Do not play a game or sport that you are not strong or fit enough to do.

- Always follow the rules of the game and encourage other members of your team to do the same.

- Wear the right gear and use the right equipment for the sport you are playing.

- Always warm up before exercise and cool down afterward.

- Never play when you are tired or in pain.

- If you play outside on hot days, wear sunscreen and a hat to prevent sunburn, and drink lots of water to prevent **dehydration.**

Rules are made to keep you safe. A careless shove in basketball could cause injuries. Referees are there to make sure that both teams follow the rules.

WHAT IF I DO NOT LIKE TEAM SPORTS?

Have you ever jumped on a trampoline, flown a kite, or walked the dog? If so, you have been getting good exercise without having to join a team or attend practices. Lots of people enjoy team sports, but there are many other ways of staying in shape.

Keep fit with a friend

When a friend comes over to play, why not take the chance to exercise? Play badminton or tennis or have races in the park. Play frisbee or catch with a softball. Work out a dance routine together or play tag. You do not have to be on a team to enjoy team sports—why not set up a soccer goal and practice your shooting and goalkeeping skills or get a baseball bat and hit some balls around?

Mark out a hopscotch grid with chalk and play with friends.

Spinning a hula hoop is a great exercise to do alone. See how many spins you can do before it falls!

Keep fit alone

There are lots of ways to exercise on your own. Go for a bike ride, set up a course to zig-zag in and out of on your rollerblades, or see how many jumps you can do with a jump rope. Set up a basket and practice shooting hoops or hit a tennis ball against a wall and work on your backhand.

PLAY IT SAFE

If you exercise outside, alone, or with a friend, play it safe.

- Tell an adult where you are going.
- Keep away from traffic. Do not play near a road—you could put yourself and others in danger.
- Never talk to strangers.
- Always go home when you said you would.

WHAT IF IT IS RAINING OUTSIDE?

Just because it is raining outside doesn't mean you can't exercise indoors and have fun. There are plenty of activities you can do indoors. Turn on some music and dance. Hop on one foot or jog in place. Try some jumping jacks or stretches.

Use a balloon to play volleyball or just hit it to keep it off the floor for as long as you can.

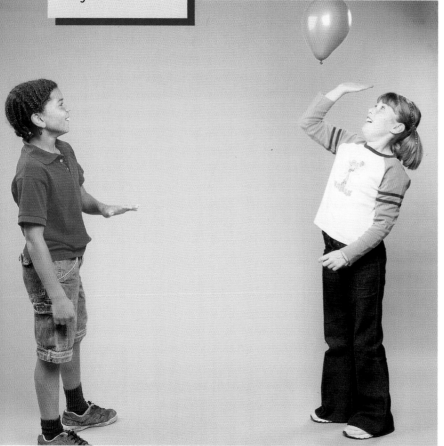

Gyms

You can also find lots of indoor exercise ideas at your local gym. When fall starts, sign up for a new class in swimming, judo, bowling, or indoor tennis. Or take up indoor rollerskating or ice skating. Whatever you choose to do—have fun and stay in shape!

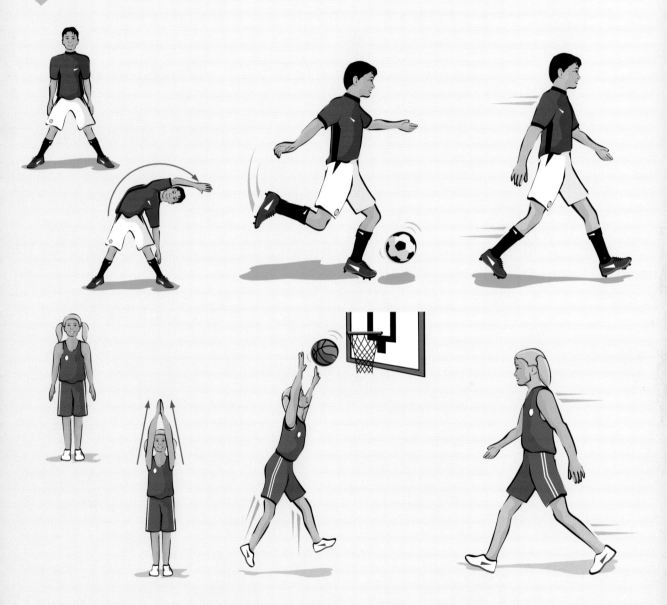

EXERCISE INFORMATION

Don't forget your warm-ups and cool-downs. In these two sets of pictures, the children are doing gentle stretches to warm up before exercise and some brisk walking to cool down afterward.

GLOSSARY

aerobic exercise exercise that makes you breathe harder. Aerobic means "needing oxygen."

artery blood vessel that carries blood from the heart to other parts of the body

blood vessel tube that carries blood around the body

bone solid body part that helps to form the skeleton that supports the soft parts of the body

carbohydrate kind of food that gives the body energy

cell smallest building block of living things

dehydrated when the body loses more water, such as by sweating, than it takes in

diaphragm muscle between the ribs and stomach

digest to break down food into nutrients to give the body energy

endorphin natural chemical in the body that is released into the blood during exercise

energy power that allows living things to do everything they need to live and grow

heart body part that pumps blood through the blood vessels

joint place where two bones join inside the body

lungs   body parts that breathe in air, taking oxygen into the body

muscle   fibers that make the different parts of the body move or do other jobs

nutrient   chemical found in food that the body needs to stay healthy

oxygen   gas in the air that you breathe in and need to live

protein   substance in some foods that the body can use to build or repair body parts

sweat   salty water that the body releases through the skin

sweat gland   part of the body that makes sweat

tendon   fiber that attaches a bone to a muscle

vitamin   substance found in food that is vital to your health

FURTHER READING

Coleman, Lori, and Jeff Savage. *Beginning Strength Training.* Minneapolis: Lerner, 1998.

Gedatus, Gus. *Exercise for Weight Management.* Mankato, Minn.: Capstone, 2000.

Sadgrove, Judy. *Exercise.* Chicago: Raintree, 1999.

Silverstein, Alvin, and Virginia B. Silverstein. *Physical Fitness.* Danbury, Conn.: Scholastic Library, 2002.

INDEX